PREPARING A ROOSTER FOR COMPETITIVE FIGHTING

PEDRO GONZALES

PEDRO GONZALES

PREPARING A ROOSTER FOR COMPETITIVE FIGHTING

3

With feathers of courage and crowns of dawn,

Roosters guard the day, their legacy drawn.

In barnyard kingdoms, they stand tall and true,

Protectors of hens, with hearts pure and blue

--Pedro Gonzales

Contents

PREPARING A ROOSTER FOR COMPETITIVE FIGHTING

Introduction

Raising roosters is a long-standing tradition in Filipino culture. It's been around for centuries, even before Magellan arrived in the Philippines in 1521. Nowadays, rooster competitions—unofficially our national sport—have become a billion-dollar industry. These events create jobs for caretakers in game farms, poultry feed factories, and cockfighting arenas where tournaments happen regularly.

As a young kid, my dad used to raise roosters in our backyard. Folks from all over—neighbors, Dad's friends, even strangers—would drop by to see the roosters. They'd chat excitedly about these birds, share laughs, and everyone seemed genuinely happy. Sometimes they'd even have friendly rooster sparring matches, eyes shining with enthusiasm and excitement.

PREPARING A ROOSTER FOR COMPETITIVE FIGHTING

It all began when I was just a kid—I got fascinated by roosters. Ever since then, I've been raising these feisty birds myself for decades. Over the years, I've picked up a wealth of knowledge about roosters and learned so much.

This book shares my perspective on raising and getting roosters ready for competitive fights. I'll take you through my experiences with these amazing birds. Think of this book as my gift to fellow rooster enthusiasts—whether they're young or old—and I hope they find valuable insights to enhance their own rooster-raising journey.

More of the Same

You know, from what I've seen, the roosters competing in today's major competitions aren't all that different from the ones that ruled the big-time derbies decades ago. Sure, there have been some minor tweaks, but they're still the fierce fighters people expect them to be—just like they were many years back. They haven't changed all that much after all.

With all these fancy new ways of getting roosters ready for battle, some folks think we've got the upper hand now compared to the past. But honestly, I don't always see it as an advantage. In my humble opinion, I'd rather stick with the conditioning methods that brought me countless victories—even if they've been around for years. Why fix what ain't broken, right? So I'll keep using the tried-and-true method I've relied on for ages.

PREPARING A ROOSTER FOR COMPETITIVE FIGHTING

Prepping a rooster for competitive fighting feels like déjà vu. You stick to the same routine because you're convinced it's what's best for your feathered warriors. Same food, same methods, same breeding—it's all on repeat. And that unwavering confidence in your roosters? It's like knowing they'll give their all, even if victory isn't guaranteed every time.

No Such Thing

Ever heard people claim that their roosters are purebred? It's a misplaced belief, but the truth is, there's no such thing as a completely purebred rooster. Different rooster breeds have diverse bloodline origins. Even if you intensely breed a specific bloodline, it won't be 100% pure. There are always traces of other bloodlines mixed in. So, purebred roosters? Not really!

Okay, so here's the deal with rooster breeds: They've been bred and rebred countless times, and sometimes they even get fancy new names based on who's doing the breeding. Now, there are definitely some top-notch rooster breeds out there, but they're still a blend of various rooster bloodlines. The real puzzle is figuring out the exact percentages of each bloodline that make up a specific breed of rooster.

PREPARING A ROOSTER FOR COMPETITIVE FIGHTING

After breeding roosters for many decades, I've noticed something interesting. We often crossbreed them with whatever bloodline we have on hand. The outcome? A mix of roosters with all sorts of different traits, making them less predictable.

I breed roosters to make them as consistent and uniform as possible. I'm not chasing after some mythical "purebred" rooster that others talk about. Instead, I aim to produce roosters that resemble each other in various ways, from fighting style to appearance, and keep doing so for as long as I can.

The Importance of Rest

When it's time to prep my roosters for a fight, I don't go overboard with strange methods. No need to panic—I stay relaxed. If I trust my approach and believe it's right, I can enjoy the process without stress.

In getting the roosters ready, I keep it simple. I focus on keeping them healthy all the time, rather than giving them special training right before a fight. It's like they're in training mode year-round.

As long as your roosters regularly engage in activities like being on a tie cord, flying pen, or running pen, and they face obstacles that challenge them, that's their training. No need for separate training sessions before a fight—they're already conditioned year-round.

But what really matters is how much rest the roosters get before a fight. Keeping their energy up is crucial, and they can only do that by getting plenty of rest, staying hydrated, and getting the right nutrients.

I've found that giving them 4 to 5 days of rest before a fight works wonders. It's pretty straightforward: pop them into the resting coops during that time and stick to their usual feed—no need for fancy diets. Oh, and don't forget to let them stretch their wings by moving them to drop pens for 15 minutes once or twice a day. Keeps 'em in tip-top shape!

Go All-Natural

I wouldn't bother with fancy stuff like performance-enhancing drugs for my roosters to win. Honestly, it's just a waste of money. Some buddies who tried them said they're pretty pricey. But even if someone handed me one for free, I'd still stick to the good ol' all-natural approach.

If you've got a top-notch rooster, why mess with enhancers? A super healthy bird doesn't need temporary synthetic performance boosts. Using enhancers feels like cheating and would tarnish your reputation as a rooster breeder and owner. So, it's a firm "no" from you!

Even though performance-enhancing drugs might boost a rooster's performance, winning isn't guaranteed. Ultimately, a rooster's natural fighting ability and a touch of luck play a significant role. Using enhancers comes with risks—misuse could hinder their innate abilities.

A rooster that's super healthy, well-rested, and comes from a winning bloodline can put up a great fight against any opponent. Roosters are born warriors; you don't need to pump them full of stuff to make them fierce—they've got it in their feathers already!

To Point, or Not to Point, That Is the Question

You know, in all my years of raising roosters and getting them ready for battle, I never really bothered with "pointing". It's just not my thing. Instead, I focus on conditioning them the way I know works best.

If you've found success with "pointing" roosters, my advice is to stick with it. We all have our own methods for conditioning them, but the ultimate goal is victory. For me, I've opted for the simpler approach.

When you're pointing your roosters, it's not a walk in the park. There are risks involved, and it's far from easy. You've got to pay close attention because pointing is all about applying scientific methods to boost your rooster's performance on fight day. But be careful—making a mistake or miscalculating can sometimes have the opposite effect!

PREPARING A ROOSTER FOR COMPETITIVE FIGHTING

I take pride in winning fights with my roosters without relying on pointing techniques. I prepare them in a way that feels right to me, focusing on their well-being. Who knows how many opponents I've beaten who used pointing methods for their birds?

Deciding whether to point your roosters or not is entirely up to you—it's all about your personal preferences. If you're okay with pointing, go ahead. But if you'd rather not bother with it, that's totally fine too. Remember, a rooster destined for victory will prevail regardless.

Keeping It Simple

In the old days, my dad would sometimes toss whole corn grains to his roosters. Those feisty birds would peck each grain right off the ground. Then he'd make sure they had fresh, clean water. But most of the time, he'd give them a mix of special grains and pellets for their regular meals. Only when he was feeling worn out would he simply scatter whole corn grains for the roosters to enjoy.

My dad's roosters look amazing! Their feathers shine bright, and they've got sturdy bodies. Whenever I watch them spar, I'm thrilled—the roosters move quickly, shuffle around, and show incredible strength. I reckon my dad's nailed the perfect feed formula; it really reflects in how the roosters both look and perform.

I've tried various poultry feeds. Some were recommended by friends, while others I experimented with myself. But you know what? Nothing compares to the good ol' basic feed for roosters: a mix of grains and pellets. I've stuck with this simple formula for a long time, and I wouldn't change it. It's a straightforward 50:50 ratio—50 percent select grains and 50 percent high-protein pellets. That's the secret sauce.

I've got about 3 or 4 types of grains I use: whole corn, barley, and wheat. Sometimes, I just mix whole corn with pellets. I serve it dry, and then let the roosters drink as much water as they want. The pellets already have some grains in them, so I'm not too concerned if it's mostly whole corn.

As long as I've got this feed mix on hand all the time, I'm good. It's got all the nutrients the roosters need daily. Anything extra would just be overkill. Honestly, the so-called secret formula isn't really a secret. It's just about keeping things simple and sticking to the basics.

Gameness

When it comes to fighting roosters, gameness is a key quality we seek. We focus on breeds that exhibit this trait and ignore those that don't. But remember, gameness isn't limited to specific breeds—every rooster breed has both quitters and those that fight to the end.

While some rooster breeds are famous for their gameness, it doesn't mean they won't back down when faced with a challenge. Gameness depends on various factors, and a rooster's breed is just one piece of the puzzle.

I've observed Asil or Oriental roosters that fight fearlessly in naked heel matches—they'll go to the bitter end. But when it comes to long knife competitions, it's a whole different ballgame. As soon as they feel the pain from deep wounds, they often flee or give up. On the other hand, some roosters in long knife battles soldier on even when their guts are spilling out, somehow pulling off a victory in the end.

Some fellow rooster enthusiasts believe that the long knife isn't the best measure of a rooster's gameness. They argue that most fights are over in just a few seconds, so the gaff competition is a more accurate test. But I respectfully disagree. In my view, the long knife is the true gauge of gameness. If a rooster can withstand lethal blows from this formidable blade, it's the real deal. The long knife sets the standard, and a survivor in long knife fights can handle any other weapon, like gaffs or short knives, with ease.

When roosters are in the heat of battle, there are a bunch of reasons why some of them just throw in the towel. Here are the main ones:

Number one is dehydration. Imagine a rooster that's super parched—like it's been wandering the desert without water. Well, a severely dehydrated rooster can't keep up the fight. It's just too weak and worn out. I've seen this happen during intense knife competitions. My own rooster, even though it was limping, toughed it out. But its opponent, also limping, just refused to peck and seemed totally out of breath. Our rooster won because the other guy didn't peck. Later, I checked the other rooster to find about its injuries. Turns out, it wasn't fatal, and my rooster was actually worse off. Also, the opponent rooster was bigger and rounder, but it looked kinda dried out. Dehydration, my friend!

Number two is sickness. If a rooster isn't feeling tip-top, it won't be in the mood for combat. It's like when you're sick—you're not up for a brawl either. So, a sick rooster just rejects anything that could harm or threaten it. Makes sense, right?

Number three is bloodline and breed. The type of rooster matters. If your bird has more Asil or Oriental blood, it might be more likely to quit in a blade fight. Bloodlines play a big role in how game a rooster is.

Investing In Raising Roosters

Raising roosters can be quite pricey. If it's your passion, it's definitely a costly pursuit. Without knowing how to recoup your investment, it might end up costing you a fortune that you can't regain.

Breeding and preparing these amazing birds for competitions can be expensive. You'll need to allocate funds from whatever source you have. It's actually quite high-maintenance.

That's why you should treat raising roosters like a business. Sell your top-quality birds to those who appreciate their value and are willing to pay your price. Give them the quality they deserve. And to build your brand, give it a unique name. Focus on breeding and raising your roosters with utmost care, as if your life depended on their success in battle.

Even if you don't compete in the major rooster derbies, consider selling your roosters to well-known industry players. I've seen serious rooster enthusiasts buy birds from small game farm owners and even backyard breeders. These buyers often purchase in bulk, and if they're happy with the results, they'll keep coming back. You could become their go-to breeder. Plus, you can still choose some of your best roosters and enter them in local fights and derbies. It's a win-win—you get to enjoy your passion and earn money. Just make sure your roosters are top-notch to attract buyers willing to pay for their excellent performance.

Importance of a Skilled Knife Handler or Gaffer

When you're getting your top roosters ready for a competition, it's essential to have a skilled knife handler or gaffer with you. Even better, learn how to attach the slasher blade or gaff to the rooster's leg yourself. Having an expert on hand during a rooster competition is a smart move.

I've noticed something interesting in rooster fights. Sometimes, even when two roosters exchange powerful blows, the one that seems to be losing ends up with only minor injuries. Meanwhile, the seemingly dominant rooster gets seriously wounded. It makes you wonder: where did all those lethal blade strikes go? Why didn't they hurt the other rooster as much?

In my many years of experience with roosters and the fights they participate in, I've noticed why some roosters don't cause as much damage to their opponents, even if they're impressive shufflers. There are a couple of reasons for this. First, it could be that the rooster isn't fully extending its leg when it delivers blows, resulting in shorter punches that lack the necessary force. Second, the position and type of blade matter. If the person handling the knife isn't skilled at positioning the blade correctly in the rooster's leg, all those impressive shuffles go to waste. A skilled knife handler would consider the rooster's fighting style. For a flyer that fights methodically, a longer blade would be appropriate. But if the rooster is a multiple shuffler and ground fighter, a shorter blade would work best.

An experienced knife handler understands where to place the blade on a rooster's leg. They can decide whether to target the heart or the liver. And they get to choose between the traditional Filipino "tari" (fork-type) method or the socket-type blade attachment.

Some of these blades are poisonous because they're soaked in cyanide. A knife expert once told me how it's done. He uses alligator clips connected to a battery. These clips attach to the blade inside a glass filled with cyanide. When he turns on the battery, electricity flows through the cyanide-soaked blade. If that blade cuts or punctures something, it creates a severe wound that damages the surrounding tissues.

Well, you see, I'm a naturalist. So, I steer clear of any sneaky tricks like putting cyanide on my rooster's blades. It's just not my style. My blades might look plain, but when they're strapped to my top fighters' legs during competitions, they pack a serious punch. Even against opponents who use cyanide-loaded blades, my roosters can break bones with their blows.

You know, the knife man or gaffer's skills play a big role in how the fight turns out. If you ignore that, you're setting yourself up for failure. And sometimes, even if your roosters could have won, they end up losing because the knife man didn't handle the blade well.

Superstitions and Success

You know, growing up in Filipino culture, I've seen how superstitions weave their way into everything—including how we raise roosters for competitions. But it's up to us to decide: do we stick with those old beliefs, or do we explore better alternatives?

When I was a kid, folks from the neighborhood would drop by our backyard to check out the roosters we had on display. They'd chat with my dad and then closely examine the roosters they were interested in. Specifically, they paid attention to the patterns on the roosters' leg scales. If they liked what they saw, they'd haggle with my dad to buy those particular roosters. My dad was happy to sell them because he saw raising roosters as both a passion and a way to make some extra income. Some folks even considered details like feather color, eye color, and tail tilt when choosing their prized roosters.

Some of these people also believe that the moon's phases can affect how well roosters perform in fights. According to their observations, when the moon is nearly full and bright, roosters with bright-colored feathers and light-colored legs tend to dominate. On the other hand, during darker moon phases, roosters with dark feathers and legs take the lead. While these superstitions sometimes hold true, they're not always reliable.

Superstitions are a personal choice. I respect those who follow them, but personally, I wouldn't base my success solely on superstitions. To me, that's like relying on luck. It's better to work hard on something you know will eventually pay off.

Selecting Roosters for Competition

When it comes to picking roosters, I'm not super picky like some other enthusiasts. I don't go all Sherlock Holmes on every little detail to find a special rooster. But I do have a few factors in mind when choosing one for a competition.

First, I'd hold the rooster with both hands and gently stretch each leg backward and forward. If the legs can extend fully in both directions, that's a good sign. Next, I'd let the rooster stand on a table or the ground. I pay attention to how it stands and the position of its legs. I prefer roosters whose bodies are clearly bent upward compared to those with only a slight upward bend from a horizontal position.

The space between the rooster's legs matters. I look for a wide gap between the legs, not a narrow one.

PREPARING A ROOSTER FOR COMPETITIVE FIGHTING

I look for roosters with rounder bodies. Near the anus (just below it), there are two parallel bones. I press my fingers near the anus area. If only one finger (or none) fits in that space, it's a good sign. Sometimes, I also consider ruddy and bright eyes, but those are secondary traits.

Choosing a rooster can be quite tricky. You're essentially making a judgment based on your own preferences and beliefs. But sometimes, even if a rooster doesn't have all the traits you were looking for, it can still surprise you by winning a competition. So, isn't that a bit of a puzzle? Ultimately, you have to trust your instincts or whatever criteria you use to select the best roosters you believe can clinch those coveted victories.

In sparring the roosters for selection, I'd look for the agile ones—those that can move quickly, take off both vertically and laterally with grace, and deliver sharp punches. If a rooster can soar high right from the start, that's even better. However, I'd avoid choosing roosters with aggressive head-hunting or straightforward fighting styles. They're more likely to get hit early in a match. And in the long knife competition, surviving a blow from a deadly blade is quite an achievement.

Top Rooster Breeds
and Winning

I bet you're curious about my most successful rooster breeds and the competitions I've entered, right? Well, let me spill the beans. The Claret-Kelso combinations have been my star players, racking up the most wins. They're like the MVPs of my flock. After them, I've got a solid lineup with Hatches, Roundheads, and Greys. I did dabble in some Dom-Lemon mixes at one point, but eventually circled back to my trusty Claret-Kelso favorites.

I've won quite a few trophies. My roosters have triumphed in both big and small derbies, as well as hack fights. Some of them even competed in major events and beat top contenders. Nowadays, I'm not actively entering my roosters in competitions; instead, I'm focused on breeding and selling them to regular clients.

Winning in rooster competitions is a huge deal. But let's not forget the sweat and effort that goes into raising these incredible birds, all the way from hatching to the cockfighting ring. Hats off to the passionate breeders and fellow rooster fans who keep the flame of this beloved sport burning.

Recently, I've been focusing on raising more grey roosters. It's like rekindling my love for them from a decade or so ago. Grey roosters have this intriguing quality, and I'm gradually uncovering their secrets. Maybe it's just rediscovering what I already knew about this breed, but it's an exciting journey.

Advice for Starting Rooster Breeding

When folks ask me for advice on starting rooster breeding, I tell them this: You've got to be all in. It's not like any other hobby where you casually invest time and effort. Breeding roosters will demand a significant chunk of your dedication and resources.

Raising roosters is like a high-stakes game. It tests your mettle—can you handle the pressure or accept the failures? Either way, you've got to persevere, just like a rooster in combat. Success hinges on navigating the process, finding that sweet spot between winning and losing. And don't forget to savor the journey—it'll take you places you never expected.

Remember those moments when you learned something valuable? Well, as you keep pushing forward, expect wins and losses. It's all part of the journey toward dominance. And sometimes your hard work won't pay off exactly as you hoped, but you can always adjust your approach if needed.

Don't forget to be kind to everyone, no matter who they are. Being generous when it really counts matters too. Sometimes, folks I know come up to me and ask if they can have a pair of my roosters and hens to breed. They can't afford to buy them, so they hope I'll just give them away. Well, I agreed. But I made sure to tell them, "Take good care of that pair, nurture them, and let them thrive." You see, kindness and generosity come in all shapes and sizes. It's not always about grand gestures; even small acts can make a difference. When we do good things for others, it sets off a positive chain reaction that impacts our lives, passions, and chosen paths—for the better.

Benefits of Raising Roosters in Mountainous Areas

Roosters raised in mountainous areas with plenty of fresh carabao grass, as long as they're well-fed and properly cared for, tend to be healthier, more robust, and have better endurance than those raised in flat plains. Young roosters can build strong leg muscles by freely roaming the hills. Additionally, high-altitude places are cooler than cities and towns on the plains. These roosters also have larger lungs because the thinner air at higher altitudes requires them to work harder to breathe in the necessary oxygen.

Having carabao grass around, along with other food sources like worms, certain plant leaves, and fallen fruit from trees, would be great for your roosters. They'll get extra nutrients from these. Also, make sure they get plenty of sunlight, but provide some shady spots too. And at night, the natural quietness will give them the refreshing rest they need.

If you can't provide fancy accommodations for your roosters, a clean and roomy backyard will do. Just make sure to fence it in so your free-range birds don't wander off into the neighborhood. It's a bit of effort, but seeing their progress will make it all worthwhile.

Get into the habit of checking on your roosters every morning while sipping your coffee or tea. Be friendly and chat with them—even though they won't reply like humans, they can feel your connection. Your presence will boost their energy and help build their confidence.

Imported vs. Local Roosters

Many rooster enthusiasts in the Philippines believe that imported roosters, especially those from the United States, are superior in quality compared to locally-produced ones. It's like a mindset leftover from colonial times, where people think anything imported is automatically better. But when it comes to roosters, that's not always true. In reality, a lot of the roosters in the Philippines—both in the past and now—have bloodlines or breeding connections to the American Game. Over the years, Filipino breeders have managed to create local versions of American Game roosters that can hold their own against the imports.

We should recognize Mamie Lacson from Bacolod City as one of the top rooster breeders in the Philippines. Back in the 1960s, Mamie acquired roosters from the legendary Harold Brown. These birds have gone on to produce offspring that perform exceptionally well in both local and international cockfighting competitions. Interestingly, the island-born American Games are proving to be hardier than their mainland counterparts.

Over the past few decades, a lot of roosters have been brought from the United States to the Philippines. As a result, most of the roosters we have here now have some American Game blood in them. These roosters are fierce fighters, and when they enter the arena, the crowd goes wild. Cockfighting is still very much alive as a sport in the Philippines, and it looks like it'll stay that way for years to come.

The Future of Cockfighting

The future of cockfighting, whether in the Philippines or anywhere else, relies on the passion and commitment of those who love the sport. While cockfighting has been banned in the United States, it's still thriving in the Philippines. Some U.S. breeders continue to raise roosters for shows, not for illegal purposes, but to preserve their bloodlines. Many American rooster enthusiasts hope that one day the ban will be lifted, allowing them to relive the golden years when cockfighting was a major part of their culture.

The Philippines has taken the crown as the ultimate hub for this particular sport. The United States banned cockfighting on their home turf, which shifted the spotlight to the Philippines. And there's no shortage of cockfighting events here. The granddaddy of them all is the 9-cock World Slasher Cup.

It's like the Super Bowl of cockfighting, happening twice a year—in January and June. The action unfolds at the swanky Araneta Coliseum in Quezon City, Metro Manila. Cockers and breeders from all corners of the globe flock to these events. It's basically the Olympics of Cockfighting.

Yes, top-notch cockers and breeders from all corners of the globe are gathering to showcase their absolute best roosters. These birds aren't just flexing their skills; they're also demonstrating their incredible endurance, fighting spirit, and exceptional qualities—even until their last breath. It's cockfighting at its finest and grandest. And you're lucky enough to witness it ringside or even have your own roosters compete and win in this epic event.

We've got these big national rooster competitions where breeders and owners from all over the country show off their top roosters. And then there are smaller local derbies in towns and cities across the Philippines, where local cockers and breeders proudly display their best birds. Plus, there are regular hack fights happening all over the country.

PREPARING A ROOSTER FOR COMPETITIVE FIGHTING

Filipinos absolutely love cockfighting. It's like their go-to pastime, a recreational sport, and even a stress-reliever. The arena is buzzing with excitement, and everyone's spirits are soaring. There's some gambling involved, but it mirrors the Filipino way of life—a constant gamble. Every day, they're betting on what matters most: survival, family, country, causes, and their unwavering beliefs.

Rooster competitions are also really taking off in Mexico and other Latin American countries. It's fascinating how our Mexican friends share similarities with us Filipinos, not just culturally but also historically. I bet they'll be leading the way in the future of cockfighting, especially when it comes to short knife matches.

Feeding Roosters Twice a Day

A fellow rooster enthusiast once asked me about a theory he'd heard: that feeding a rooster once a day might be better than twice a day. Initially, I didn't take it too seriously and tried to change the subject. But when he persisted, I shared my thoughts based on my experience raising roosters and some common sense.

I explained that a fighting rooster benefits from two meals a day. In the morning, it gets the energy it needs for the day's activities (whether it's fighting or other tasks). Then, in the afternoon, it replenishes any lost nutrients. If you only feed it once a day, it might miss out on essential nutrients and have less reserve energy, potentially leading to low metabolism.

Feeding your roosters twice a day is the sweet spot. Going below or above that might not be great for their overall health. And don't forget to slip in some small snacks between meals to keep their metabolism humming.

When you're fasting your roosters for deworming, be careful not to completely withhold water. Depriving them of water for too long can be risky. Initially, it might lead to dehydration, and later on, it could even cause auto-intoxication.

My rooster-loving friend was pretty impressed with my rooster know-how. I just told him that when you're all about roosters and spend loads of time with them, you pick up things naturally over time. Experience works its magic not only in raising roosters but in everything else too.

Knowing When to Quit

Sometimes, no matter how much effort you put into breeding and raising roosters—making sure everything's just right—it feels like everything crumbles. The harder you try, the closer you get to failure. So, when's the right time to throw in the towel? Honestly, it's a tough question, especially when you're passionate about something. How do you quit when it's something you care so deeply about?

When you find yourself stuck in a rut, despite giving it your all, consider taking a breather. It's not quitting; think of it as hitting the pause button when things aren't going your way. Take that time to reflect. Once everything sinks in, you'll see the bigger picture. Then, decide whether you want to stage a comeback and keep raising roosters or step away for good. It's your call.

PREPARING A ROOSTER FOR COMPETITIVE FIGHTING

Failure happens to all of us—it's just part of life. We've all stumbled at some point, maybe even more than once. Some failures teach us valuable lessons, while others are tough to swallow. But no matter how we handle them, remember this: they're only temporary.

We're the captains of our own ships. When to keep sailing and when to drop anchor—it's all in our hands. Whether we're charting a course toward success or steering into rough waters, it's our choices that set the sails.

Rooster Competition Prep

When you're getting your prized roosters ready for those intense competitions, don't forget about yourselves. Yep, that's right— the owners and handlers need to be in tip-top shape too. The night before the big showdown, make sure you catch some quality sleeps. And tell your handlers to do the same. You want everyone waking up refreshed and raring to go in the morning. And if you've got long hair, consider a fresh trim. And those thick beards and mustaches? Time to shave 'em off. It's like clearing the path for maximum energy flow. Let's get battle-ready.

Your roosters are like little energy sponges. They soak up vibes from you and the people around you. Now, we want those vibes to be positive—like a sunny day at the farm, not a stormy one.

Roosters can actually recognize your unique scent. It's like their secret handshake with you. But if you suddenly switch perfumes right before a big cockfight, it's like changing the password to their WiFi. They might get a bit confused and lose that connection they're used to having with you.

It sounds a bit superstitious. But there's probably some science behind it. Maybe it's all about pheromones or energy fields. Who knows? The important thing is, you've been doing this dance with your roosters, and it's been a success.

Roosters feel more confident when you're around. They soak up positive vibes from you, which boosts their own energy. And right before a cockfight, you can give your rooster a friendly pat on the back of its head and offer some encouraging words. Think of yourself as a general checking in on your troops before battle, motivating them for what lies ahead.

Peruvian-American Roosters: Hype vs. Reality

Once upon a time, Peruvian roosters took the Philippines by storm. Local breeders got all fired up and started crossbreeding them with Island-born American Games. Their goal? To create a winning combination that could dominate in long knife competitions. These Peruvian-American hybrids became so popular that their price skyrocketed—a trio of the original Peruvian breeds could set you back a hefty $4,000 to $5,000. Compare that to importing a trio of good American Games, which would only cost around $1,500 to $2,000.

But despite the hype, these fancy roosters aren't raking in the victories at prestigious national and international derbies. Where did they go wrong?

Peruvian roosters are truly impressive fighters. When you watch them in action, it's captivating to see how they take down their opponents. However, the original Peruvian breeds are massive—like the giants of the rooster world. They're much bigger than American Games. Because of this size difference, they can't be fairly matched up in competitions. So, breeders have their work cut out for them—balancing size, fighting ability, and gameness to create top-notch contenders. Now, there are hybrid Peruvian breeds that can still fight like the originals, but they don't dominate in long knife competitions as some of them struggle with gameness.

Favorite Rooster Breed:
Claret-Kelso Mix

With all the rooster breeds making waves in competitions these days—both locally and internationally—I've got a recommendation for you. Drawing from my decades of experience breeding and raising roosters, I've seen it all: breeds coming and going, making comebacks, and sometimes fading away only to rise again. But there's one combo that stands out—the Claret-Kelso mix. It's my absolute favorite. This bloodline has brought me more victories than any other rooster breed I've ever raised.

The Claret breed of rooster is quite remarkable. These birds are known for their agility, toughness, and strength. Their naturally robust bodies and compact build make them exceptionally strong, providing the stability they need to deliver powerful blows.

Now, the Kelso breed is a different story.
These roosters are both smart and ferocious
fighters. They also boast strong bodies and a
fierce spirit. When you combine the Claret
and Kelso bloodlines, you've got yourself a
precious gem—a rooster with the best of
both worlds.

Rooster Breeds and Fighting Styles

Although I really love Claret-Kelso roosters, that doesn't mean other breeds aren't great. Let me tell you about some of my other favorite fighting rooster breeds, their personalities, attributes, and fighting style.

The **Lemon 84** rooster is pretty smart in the ring. It's got this uncanny timing that helps it dodge attacks and deliver knockout blows with just one stroke. Plus, it's a pro at sidestepping and counterattacking. These guys come from Bacolod and usually kick butt against newer breeds. Look for the ones with lemon-colored feathers, straight or pea combs, and yellow or green legs.

Roundheads are a type of rooster originally from Asia. They have small, pea-shaped combs and black spurs. You'll often find them with yellow or white legs, red eyes, and pale-yellow feathers around their necks.

PREPARING A ROOSTER FOR COMPETITIVE FIGHTING

These clever fighters are great at dodging attacks and moving sideways because of their natural agility. When it comes to fighting, their aggressive and lightning-fast style makes them tough opponents, especially in aerial battles.

Brown Reds are really agile roosters. They're known for showing off with their fancy moves during fights. Picture them strutting around with dark legs and intense eyes. But they get tired easily. So, they're not the best for long battles. Breeders got smart, though. They mixed Brown Reds with Asil and other tough breeds to boost their stamina. If you want a quick, efficient fighter in your coop, the Brown Red is your guy.

Sweaters are tough roosters that fight until their opponents give up. They pack a serious punch, taking down other roosters with relentless attacks. Sweaters used to get tired easily, but breeders figured out a solution: they mixed in some other bloodlines. Now, they're known for their strength and feared in cockfights. Whether it's an aerial duel or a ground battle, Sweaters keep attacking until their rivals surrender.

Hatch roosters, similar to Whitehackle roosters, are highly respected among breeders. These birds are famous for their fighting spirit, strength, and aggressiveness. What sets them apart is their big, muscular bodies. You can't miss their bright red heads and slightly wider combs. Hatches grow up fast, with sturdy bodies and strong bones. Rain or shine, they stay in top shape. Some popular strains include the Yellow-legged hatch, Morgan hatch, Blueface hatch, and McLean hatch.

Whitehackle breed of roosters are considered some of the most beautiful breeds by many breeders. They have straight combs, stand tall with broad shoulders, and sport a compact build covered in thick plumage. Most Whitehackle roosters are red with mustard-colored hackles, although some show off a majestic white color.

Despite their good looks, Whitehackles are fierce fighters. They're known for their high gameness (that eagerness to fight) and their exceptional intelligence. Breeders often call them "ring generals" because they're savvy in the fighting ring. They strategically position themselves and move with agility.

Whitehackles aren't just brains; they're brawns too. They pack a punch and have excellent cutting ability. Plus, they're tough and durable, able to withstand hits and go the distance in drag fights. Some popular Whitehackle bloodlines include the Morgan Whitehackle and the Kearney Whitehackle. So, if you're into aesthetics and want a smart, strong fighter, Whitehackle is the breed for you.

Regular Greys are a type of rooster that comes from mixing three different grey rooster families in a breeding program: the Law Grey, the Sweater Grey, and the Plainhead Muff Grey. These Regular Greys usually have green legs, sometimes with yellow coloring, silver duck wings, and a straight comb. They're medium to low in height and are known for their strength and fighting spirit. Many breeders consider them just as powerful and determined as the Bluefaces. Because of this, a lot of breeders use Regular Greys as the foundation for crossbreeding with other rooster breeds.

Butchers are a type of rooster known for their precise fighting skills. Experts often say, "When a Butcher hits you, you're really hit". These roosters are usually medium to low in height. Some Butchers have spangled or brassback feathers, and the ones with black feathers are called Black Butchers. They typically have red feathers and can be white-legged or yellow-legged. Phil Marsh is the mastermind behind the Butcher bloodline, which combines Grove WhiteHackle and Spanish fowl called Speeder Greys. Interestingly, Phil Marsh fought under the name 'Butcher Boys' due to his occupation.

PREPARING A ROOSTER FOR COMPETITIVE FIGHTING

The Rooster's Unyielding Heart

*I wrote this poem recently, and it's all about
how much I appreciate roosters and how
they're a lot like us. Hope you enjoy it.*

In the heart of a scorching arena,
where dust swirls and the crowd
buzzes with excitement,
a rooster stands ready.
Its feathers gleam
like molten copper,
a tribute to its long lineage.

With eyes as sharp as its talons,
the rooster sizes up its opponent—
a mirror image of defiance.
The air crackles with anticipation,
and the crowd leans in,
holding their breath.

PEDRO GONZALES

This rooster embodies courage,
etched into its lean body
through countless battles
under sunrises and moonlit nights.

It knows no fear, no surrender.
Its chest swells with determination,
and its red comb stands tall
against all odds.

Ferocity pulses through its veins,
a primal force defying reason.

When the first gong sounds,
it lunges, wings slicing the air like blades.
Feathers scatter, and the ground trembles.

Agility is its secret weapon—
a lightning-fast dance of strikes
and evasive moves.
It sidesteps danger
with the grace of a matador,
feathers trailing like silk ribbons.

The crowd gasps, caught in the whirlwind
of its movements.
And that fighting spirit—
the molten core fueling its every heartbeat—
it remembers the hands that raised it,
the whispered promises of victory.

PREPARING A ROOSTER FOR
COMPETITIVE FIGHTING

In that sacred moment,
it fights not just for itself
but for the bond
forged in sweat and trust.

When the final blow lands,
the rooster stands victorious,
chest heaving, eyes ablaze.

The crowd erupts, their voices
merging into a primal roar.
They've witnessed more than a battle;
they've glimpsed life's essence.

So, under the relentless sun, the rooster
reigns—
a feathered gladiator, a symbol of toughness,
a tribute to the indomitable spirit within us
all.

Long after the dust settles,
its crow echoes through time,
a clarion call honoring
the fierce heart that beats
in each of us.

62

PREPARING A ROOSTER FOR COMPETITIVE FIGHTING

PEDRO GONZALES

PREPARING A ROOSTER FOR COMPETITIVE FIGHTING